STUFF + MUTTS = AWESOME

CHRONICLE BOOKS
SAN FRANCISCO

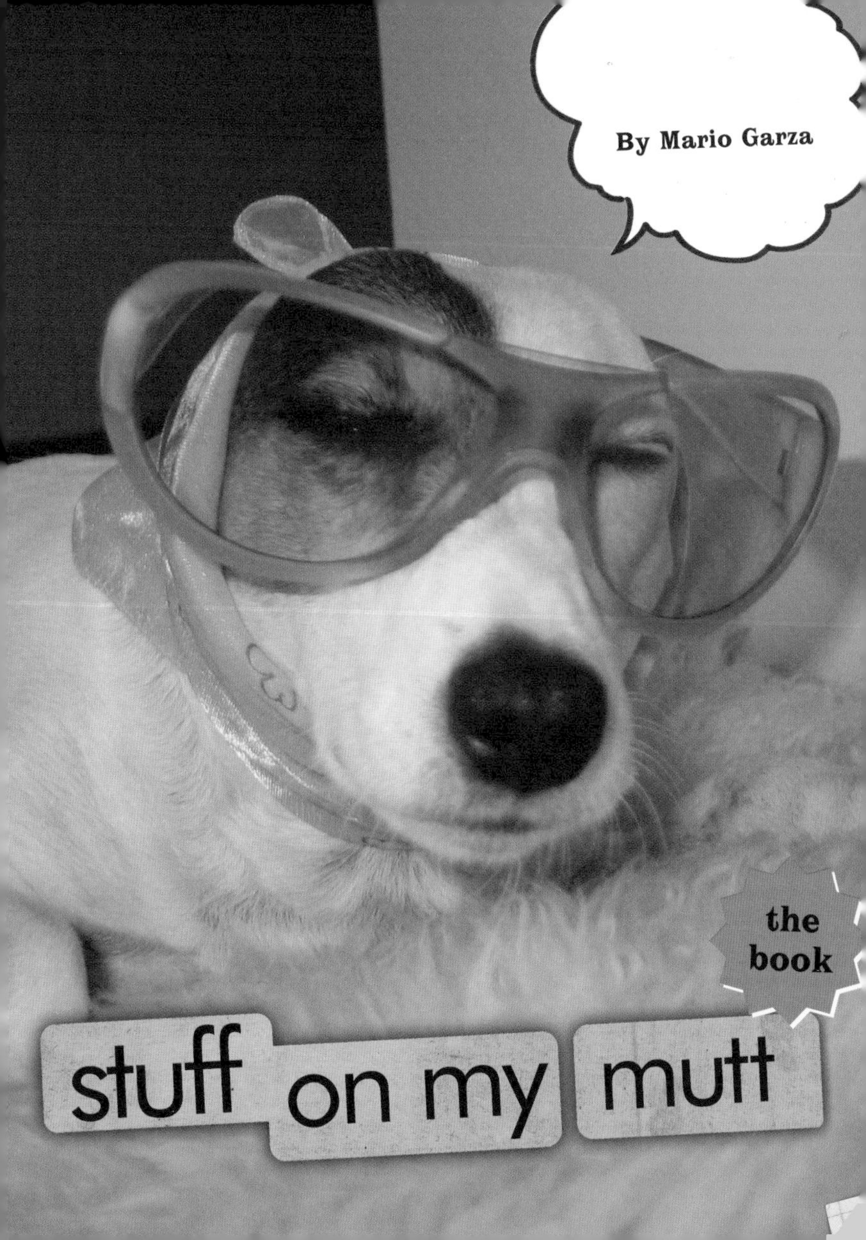
By Mario Garza
the book
stuff on my mutt

Library of Congress Cataloging-in-Publication Data available.

ISBN 978-0-8118-6897-6

Manufactured in China.
Drawings by Deth P. Sun
Design & handlettering by Benjamin Shaykin & Nico Shaykowitz

10 9 8 7 6 5 4 3 2

Chronicle Books LLC
680 Second Street
San Francisco, California 94107

www.chroniclebooks.com

As the years pass, it's slowly being replaced with "That cat guy." With friendly introductions I've gone from "This is my friend Mario," to "This is that cat guy I was telling you about." For an obsessed cat person this may not be so bad, but for a easygoing owner like myself it's a bit misleading. Fortunately for me, it's only in a very small circle where I hear this. Unfortunately, that circle happens to include *every* person I know. Where did this branding come from and why am I talking about cats in a dog book? Let's step into the Way Back Machine and take a psychedelic journey all the way to the spring of 2005.

In April 2005 I created a humor site that would unknowingly nudge me into "that cat guy" status among my peers. On a whim and without much planning, I started StuffOnMyCat.com. The initial idea came to me after I discovered I wasn't the only person to place random objects on their cat while it is sleeping. The site launched with a few pictures and a simple request: Send me your stuff-on-cat photos. It didn't take long before thousands of pictures flooded my inbox from around the globe. Millions of people visited, and before you knew it a community was born. Dog owners, however, were feeling left out in the rain. Pretty soon they were asking for a site of their very own.

They wanted a place where they could be free to dress up ol' poochy in a mime outfit and take photos of their mutts wearing wigs, a place where they wouldn't be persecuted for putting red pumps on their pug. They wanted a place where their stuff-on-dog behavior is not only accepted but also where it's encouraged and, more important, rewarded.

In March of 2007, we launched StuffOnMyMutt.com. Our mission: to compromise the dignity of another species. I don't like to name-drop, but when asked about the site, my mother once said, "It's the pinnacle achievement in human/canine relations." The format was the same, the humor was identical, and without fail overly obsessed pet owners from around the globe participated.

When we put out the call for stuff-on-mutt photos, we had no idea what kind of submissions we would receive. We were both shocked and slightly embarrassed at what some dogs were willing to tolerate for a good photo. The following pages represent some of the best photos we've received over the last two and a half years. I don't want to sound arrogant, but with these images occupying space in your library, I think it's safe to say your book collection is now complete. Don't forget to visit the site and get your dog in on the stuff-on-mutt action. Who knows, perhaps your pooch will grace these pages one day.

—Mario "That Cat Guy" Garza

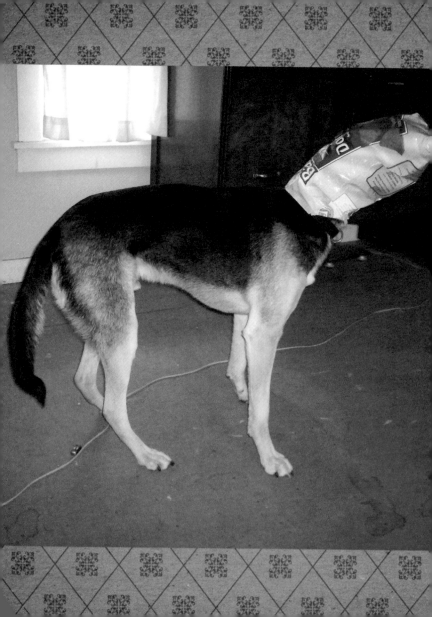

--- *I'm a* ---

MANIAC,

-- *maaaniac!*

BARRY

Snyder's hobbies include raves, Mardi Gras, New Year's, and any occasion that allows him to wear a funky wig!

SUP GIRL,
you come here often?

PARKER

The only
three friends
I can
depend on.

and for my next trick . . .

This is our revenge for Apollo destroying and eating the following over the course of the last year: 1 table, 2 chairs, 1 can cocoa mix, 1 chocolate pie (with wrapper), 2 ottomans, 3 speakers, 4 DVDs, 1 fire hose, most of my women's underwear, 1 Willie Nelson record, 1 pair scissors, 2 pot holders. All this, and the only thing that has made him feel bad is putting a pumpkin hat on his head!

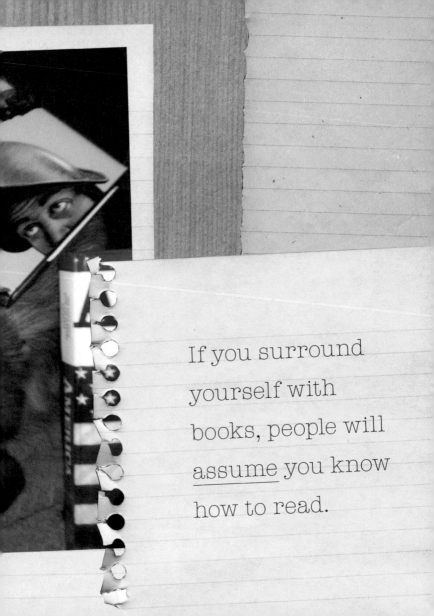

If you surround
yourself with
books, people will
<u>assume</u> you know
how to read.

OTTO

Consider your bank account officially hacked.

The Mushroom Kingdom has been infiltrated!

HOBBS

BUDDY

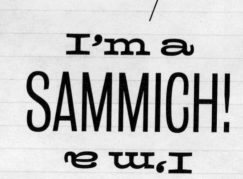

There goes my
bad boy reputation.

I'm borderline
obsessed.
There, I said it.

I may or may not have eaten one of your decorations.

Are the bad people gone yet?

Let's get together and feel all right . . .

The lady at the mall said these are all the rage these days.

CLYDE

It took me eight years, but I finally did it!

MUTTLI

All we
need is a
few stamps
and we'll
be on
our way.

But I don't know how to dwum.

Angie went where no collie has gone before.
She mingled with Vulcans, Bajorans, all kinds of Starfleet
officers, and even managed a Tribble Trouble.

TANK

Good news guys . . . I got the job!

Are Christmas trees really that expensive now?

You ruined my hair and you ruined my prom!

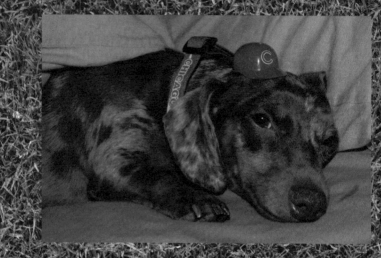

Come back aliens,
come rescue me.

Don't forget
the sauerkraut.

Guys want me and g
wanna be me.

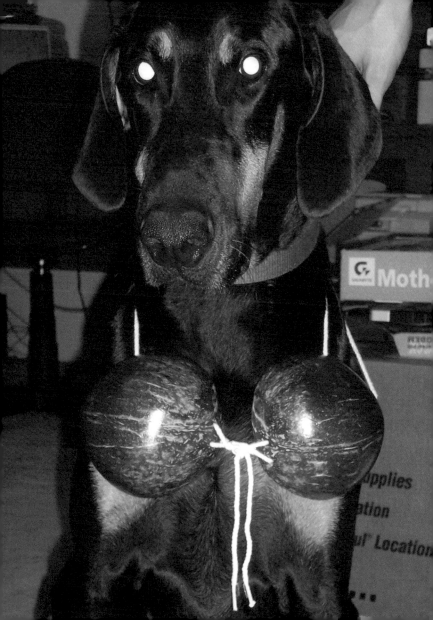

These butterflies think they're so smart.

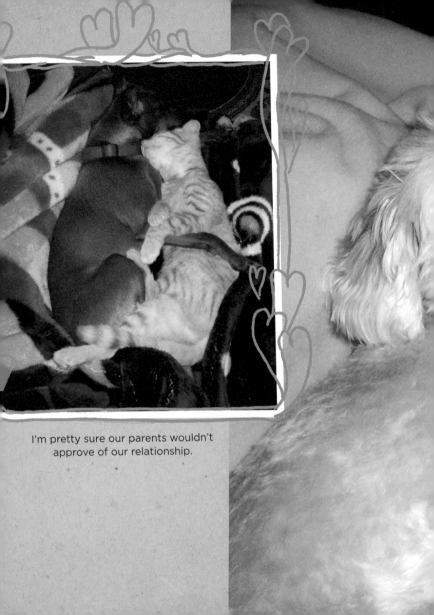

I'm pretty sure our parents wouldn't
approve of our relationship.

HUGGY
BEAR

This is my serious face.

Looking for the dog who peed on the carpet?
I'm afraid I have no idea what you're talking about.

PDRO

AND

somehow

—— HE'S STILL ON THE PAYROLL.

MALCOLM

Does this dress
make me look fat?

All of the fame went straight to her head.

TEX

This picture better not
end up on MySpace . . .

WARP SPEED

or

NO SPEED.

The prehistoric doggysaurus seen in his natural habitat.

I got expelled from clown school . . . *sniffle*

Think of it as a food funnel. Toss some treats in my general direction and I'll do the rest.

MALARKEY

It's been a loooong week.

DEDICATION

This book is dedicated to the feline who started it all—
the calico from Calcot, the queen of queens, the
long-haired legend—Love. Rest in peace old friend,
1993–2008.

Mario Garza is a freelance graphic designer, blogger, and
student. He recently traded the California sun for the overcast
skies of Portland, Oregon. Inspired by his pets' laziness he
created Stuff On My Cat in the spring of 2005 and Stuff On My
Mutt in early 2007. If you like this book, you might like his other
two, *Stuff on My Cat* and *More Stuff on My Cat* published by
Chronicle Books.